Tecumseh
Leader

Written by D. L. Birchfield
Illustrated by Murv Jacob

MODERN CURRICULUM PRESS

Program Reviewers

Cathy White Eagle, Executive Director
and President of the Board
Eagle Vision Educational Network
Granite Bay, California

Gwen Sebastian Hill, Teacher
Development Trainer
District of Philadelphia
Philadelphia, Pennsylvania

Joan Webkamigad, Education Specialist
Michigan Department of Education
Lansing, Michigan

Jeffrey Hamley, Director
Native American Program
Harvard University
Cambridge, Massachusetts

Paulette Molin, Ph.D., Assistant Dean
The Graduate College
Hampton University
Hampton, Virginia

Executive Editor: Janet Rosenthal
Project Editors: Elizabeth Wojnar
Mark Shelley

MODERN CURRICULUM PRESS

An imprint of Paramount Supplemental Education
250 James Street
Morristown, New Jersey 07960

ISBN 0-8136-5762-8 (Reinforced Binding)   0-8136-5768-7 (Paperback)
Library of Congress Catalog Card Number: 94-077295

10 9 8 7 6 5 4 3 2 1   SP   99 98 97 96 95 94

Dear Reader,

This is the story of Tecumseh. Tecumseh was a great leader of the Shawnee Nation.

As a boy, Tecumseh loved to listen to stories. He hoped one day to help his people.

When Tecumseh grew up, he continued to listen and learn. He traveled to other Native American Nations. He wanted the nations to work together as one.

As you read about Tecumseh, try to remember stories you have heard that have taught you something important.

Your friend,

Don Birchfield

One night in 1768, a shooting star
flashed across the sky. That same
night, a boy was born into the
Shawnee Nation. His name was
Tecumseh.

Tecumseh was born into a family of leaders. His father, grandfather, and great-grandfather had all been great Shawnee chiefs. Everyone hoped that Tecumseh would also be a chief.

3

When Tecumseh was born, the Shawnee lived on land that is now part of the states of Ohio, Illinois, Indiana, and Kentucky. Tecumseh had an older brother and sister, as well as three younger brothers. These younger brothers were triplets, which means that they all had been born at the same time.

In Tecumseh's village, the older and wiser people, or elders, helped parents raise the children. Before long, the elders noticed that Tecumseh was a very fast learner. As a baby, he learned quickly when it was important to be quiet. Crying or making loud noises could guide an enemy directly to him.

As a child, Tecumseh learned about
the history of the Shawnee people
from his father. Whenever
Tecumseh's father returned home
from a trip, he would share stories
about his travels.

Tecumseh also liked to hunt. He became an expert with a bow and arrow. He used his hunting skills to help provide food for his village.

Tecumseh liked games, too. He often led the other children as they played.

When Tecumseh was a teenager,
he traveled to the edge of the
buffalo plains with his older
brother, Chiksika. They visited
their friends from other Native
American nations.

For more than a year, Tecumseh and
Chiksika traveled and hunted. Along the
way, they learned about many other
Native American nations.

But it was a time of trouble in the
United States. Settlers were moving west.
They took the land that Native Americans
had always lived on. This made the
Native Americans very angry. They
fought long and hard to keep their
land. But the Native Americans
were losing the fight.

Tecumseh, now a young man, had become a great warrior, or fighter. He wanted to protect the people of his nation. He had a plan that could stop the settlers from taking Shawnee land. Tecumseh wanted the Native American nations to work together.

Tecumseh visited many Native American
nations. In 1811, he traveled to the
Chickasaw, Choctaw, and Creek nations.

Tecumseh was a great speaker. After
listening to him, many Native Americans
agreed that all Native American nations
should work together as one.

18

19

Before long, many Native Americans were talking about Tecumseh and his plan. While some joined him, others did not. Some Native Americans felt that joining Tecumseh would only cause more fighting with the settlers. Many Native Americans had grown tired of the fighting and the killing.

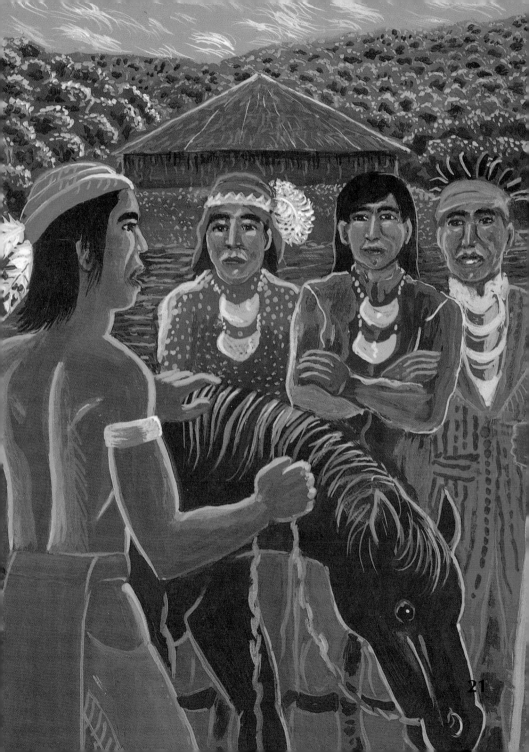

Before Tecumseh could join together with many Native Americans, the War of 1812 began. This war was between the Americans and the British.

Tecumseh joined the British army. He thought that if his people helped the British win the war, the British would share the land with them.

Tecumseh fought bravely in the war. He became sad when he realized that the British were losing. Then, on October 5, 1813, Tecumseh was killed in battle. His dream of joining together the Native American nations died with him.

Some believe Tecumseh's dream might have come true if he had more time. Others believe that the Americans, who had better weapons, would have outnumbered the Native Americans. But most agree that Tecumseh was one of the greatest Native American leaders of all time.

Glossary

elder (el′dər) an older person who is very wise

expert (eks′pərt) a person who has special skill in something

nation (na′shən) a group of people who live under the same government

settler (set′lər) a person who moves to a new place to live

triplet (trip′lət) one of three children who are born at the same time and who have the same mother

About the Author

D. L. Birchfield is an enrolled member of the Choctaw Nation of Oklahoma. He has a law degree from the University of Oklahoma College of Law, and is a student of Native American history. Mr. Birchfield believes that it is important that children get accurate and authentic information about Native American cultures and leaders. He is currently working on a book and a play for children.

About the Illustrator

Murv Jacob is a painter and pipemaker of Kentucky Cherokee and European ancestry. He has received many awards for his paintings and clay pipes, and he has illustrated more than twenty-five books. Mr. Jacob lives in Tahlequah, Oklahoma with his wife, Debbie, and their four children. In *Tecumseh,* Mr. Jacob used bright colors and detail to portray the life of the Shawnee leader.